SUMMITING EVEREST

HOW A PHOTOGRAPH CELEBRATES TEAMWORK AT THE TOP OF THE WORLD

by Emma Carlson Berne

Content Adviser: Olivia Sofer, Certified Guide
Association of Canadian Mountain Guides

COMPASS POINT BOOKS
a capstone imprint

Compass Point Books are published by Capstone,
1710 Roe Crest Drive, North Mankato, Minnesota 56003
www.capstonepub.com

Editor: Catherine Neitge
Designer: Tracy Davies McCabe
Media Researcher: Wanda Winch
Library Consultant: Kathleen Baxter
Production Specialist: Kathy McColley

Image Credits
Capstone: 49; Corbis: Reuters, 52; Royal Geographic Society: Alfred Gregory, cover,
6, 7, 9, 14, 16, 17, 22, 29, 33, 35, 37, 38, 41, 46, 53, 57 (bottom), 58, 59 (bottom
left), Anon, 5, 56, Charles Wylie, 27, 59 (top right), Edmund Hillary, 25, 28, 44, 48,
50, George Band, 19, George Lowe, 30, 43, 47, 54, Indian Air Force, 36, J.B. Noel,
11, 57 (top), John Hunt, 13, 59 (top left), Michael Westmacott, 21

Library of Congress Cataloging-in-Publication Data
Berne, Emma Carlson.
Summiting Everest : how a photograph celebrates teamwork at the top of the world/
by Emma Carlson Berne.
  pages cm.—(Compass Point Books. Captured history.)
  Includes bibliographical references and index.
  ISBN 978-0-7565-4734-9 (library binding)
  ISBN 978-0-7565-4790-5 (paperback)
  ISBN 978-0-7565-4796-7 (ebook PDF)
1. Hillary, Edmund, 1919–2008—Portraits. 2. Tenzing Norgay, 1914–1986—Portraits.
3. Mountaineering expeditions—Everest, Mount (China and Nepal)—Pictorial works.
4. Portrait photography—Everest, Mount (China and Nepal) I. Title.

Printed in the United States of America in Stevens Point, Wisconsin.
092013   007773WZS14

TABLEOFCONTENTS

ChapterOne
OPENING A HIDDEN WORLD

Boots crunched in the snow. Lungs labored to draw breath. Muscles fought against utter exhaustion. Thousands of feet below in the valleys of Nepal, flowers bloomed in the spring sunshine, and leaves waved gently in the afternoon breeze. People went about their placid daily lives in the sun-washed villages.

But for the climbers on Mount Everest, the world was reduced to a few simple elements: snow, ice, rock, wind. Beneath them spread the vast yawning crevasses and sheer rock faces of the Himalayas. Above them rose the summit of Mount Everest. That triangular pyramid, with its familiar plume of condensation whipping from the peak, was only about 1,000 feet (305 meters) away. But no one in recorded history had ever reached it and returned alive. Edmund Hillary and Tenzing Norgay wanted to be the first.

Since 8:45 that morning, May 28, 1953, Hillary and Norgay and their support team of Alfred Gregory, George Lowe, and Ang Nyima had been climbing from a high camp on the mountain. Below them, at the lower camps, the rest of the British expedition waited anxiously. They had been on the mountain since April 12. Two team members had failed to reach the summit two days ago. Now another pair's chance had come.

In 1856 the Great Trigonometrical Survey of British

> For the climbers on Mount Everest, the world was reduced to a few simple elements: snow, ice, rock, wind.

Everest was named after George Everest, a surveyor general of India. It is known as Chomolungma in Tibet (mother goddess of the universe) and Sagarmatha in Nepal (goddess of the sky).

India mapped Mount Everest and found that, at just over 29,000 feet (8,840 m), it was the highest place on Earth. Ever since then, climbers and adventurers had regarded the mountain with wonder and awe. Would it be possible to climb it? Could a person make it all the way to the top and, quite literally, stand on top of the world?

A British expedition trekked to Everest in 1921 to examine the mountain and try to determine a route to the top. Another expedition tried to climb the mountain the next year—and failed. Other expeditions tried and failed in 1924, 1933, 1936, 1938, and 1952. The mountain was

Edmund Hillary (left) and Tenzing Norgay climb toward the waiting support team at 27,300 feet (8,320 m).

proving a formidable opponent.

Now, on this May afternoon, the team of Brits, New Zealanders, and Sherpas would try to be the first to send climbers to the top of Mount Everest—and have them return alive.

Support team members George Lowe, Sherpa Ang Nyima, and team photographer Alfred Gregory had been working their way up the mountain since morning, preparing the way for Edmund Hillary and Tenzing Norgay—the assault team. Each was carrying a load of 65 pounds (30 kilograms)—the heaviest loads that have ever been carried that high. All morning Lowe and Gregory had cut steps into the crusted snow with ice axes so Hillary and Norgay could have easier footing when they followed later that day. The support team wouldn't have the glory of making the assault attempt, but they didn't mind. In 2007 Gregory told *Australian Geographic* magazine, "It has often been asked, why didn't we [the support team] then go to the top the next day? ... In those days the whole idea was to get somebody on top. It was a team effort and we did just that!"

Hillary and Norgay—a New Zealand beekeeper and a Tibetan mountain guide—climbed up to meet the support team at midday. The pair needed to find a place to camp for the night. The next morning they would try for the summit, but in the meantime they needed to rest, sleep, and eat to gather their strength.

But the slope was very steep and the team could not find a place flat enough for a tent. In his book *The Picture of Everest,* Alfred Gregory—or Greg, as he was often called—wrote, "For a long time the ridge ran remorselessly upwards without hope of a platform for a tent. ... But eventually we did find a place, a slightly outward-sloping ledge, at a height of 27,900 feet, and there at 3 o'clock in the afternoon George Lowe, Ang Nyima and I turned to go down, leaving Ed Hillary and Tenzing to their lonely vigil of the night of May 28th."

But Gregory does not mention something else he did before heading down the mountain. He pulled a small

Hillary (left) and Norgay moments before being left alone on the mountain

camera from under his down suit and snapped a quick picture: Hillary and Norgay on the rocky slope of Everest, the Himalayas spread behind them in all their vast, snowy glory. It was the highest any photographer had ever taken a picture.

For six weeks the team had been alone in the hidden world of Everest. Only they had seen the dangerous beauty of the deep-blue ice crevasses and the brilliant sun reflecting off the smooth snow. Only they had seen the Sherpas climbing ladders while carrying loads affixed to their bodies by headbands. With a click of his camera's shutter, Gregory opened this hidden world for the rest of humanity to share.

As he wrote in the introduction to *The Picture of Everest:* "Neither I nor the pictures themselves can tell much of the struggle in the rarified air, or the unbelievable fatigue that can come to a climber toiling up the last slopes of the mountain, where he almost reaches the end of human endurance and lives at the physical limit of possible life; but these pictures will perhaps bring you nearer to our adventure, and say a little of why men climb."

THE DEADLY SUMMIT ATTEMPT

Two members of the 1924 British team, Andrew Irvine (back row, left) and George Mallory (back row, second from left), never returned.

Before Edmund Hillary and Tenzing Norgay, a British team attempted the summit of Everest—and never returned. In 1924 Englishmen George Mallory and Andrew "Sandy" Irvine and the rest of the British expedition had been on Everest far longer than they had intended. They were tired and cold. Members of the team had twice tried to reach the top but had been forced to retreat. One of them, T. Howard Somervell, was coughing up the mucous lining of his larynx. But Mallory was still determined to climb. He had already been on two other expeditions to Everest. This time he was determined to make the summit.

He chose Sandy Irvine as a companion. Even though the young man had no high-altitude climbing experience, Irvine was brilliant at fixing the essential but trouble-prone oxygen equipment. As planned, Sherpas helped Mallory and Irvine get settled, then left them at their camp June 7. The next day another member of the team, Noel Odell, was gazing at the upper reaches of the mountain from a lower camp. He saw two figures appear near a rock band that Mallory had said they would cross. Odell only spied the tiny men for a moment, and then drifting clouds hid them.

Mallory and Irvine were never heard from again. For a long time, no one knew what had happened to the climbers. No one could find their bodies. Did they reach the summit, only to be killed on the descent? Or did they fall or freeze on the way up? Finally in 1999 an American team found Mallory's frozen body near the dead climbers' final camp. Mallory had a broken leg and injuries to his head and the right side of his body. He had suffered a fatal fall. No sign of Irvine has ever been found. In the years since, most researchers have concluded that Mallory and Irvine never reached the summit. Some still hope they did, but no definitive evidence either way has ever been found.

ChapterTwo
A CRACK AT EVEREST

After George Mallory and Sandy Irvine died on Everest in 1924, there were no more expeditions for almost a decade. Another attempt by the British in 1933 was a failure, with the team worn down by the altitude and hallucinating invisible companions and pulsating objects in the sky. Other attempts during the 1930s got no higher.

But once World War II was over, the British were ready to try for the summit again. And they had a new route to try. Earlier expeditions had climbed Everest from the north, starting in Tibet. But now, with the shifting postwar political landscape, Tibet was closed to outsiders. On the other hand, Nepal, which had been closed to foreigners for decades, was now opening its borders. Members of an exploratory expedition thought the Everest summit could be approached from a new direction—the south, starting in Nepal.

But just as today, an expedition could not climb Everest without a permit issued by the government—in this case, the government of Nepal. Only one group was allowed on the mountain per year. And it just so happened that a Swiss team had applied for a permit right before the British. They had first crack at the summit. If they succeeded, they would receive the worldwide acclaim that came with being the first team to climb Everest. Only if they failed would the British have a shot.

Tenzing Norgay atop a peak in Nepal

In 1952 the Swiss expedition began its trek up the mountain. One of its members was a man who would soon have a very important place in history: Tenzing Norgay. He was a Sherpa, a member of a Himalayan ethnic group living in Tibet and Nepal. Sherpas have lived for hundreds of years in a group of valleys at the base of the slopes of Mount Everest. For centuries the Sherpas in this rugged region had farmed, herded yaks, and traded goods. But Sherpa culture changed forever in 1921 when the British took their first expedition to Mount Everest.

Sherpas, including one carrying a tree trunk to be fashioned into a ladder, make their way up the mountain in April 1953.

They climbed higher than any known human had ever climbed before. But they were forced to turn around.

The British teams needed helpers to tend the mountain camps and carry the massive amounts of gear required to support life high on Everest. The Sherpa people were used to living at a very high altitude and weren't as affected by the thin air as the Europeans. And so on almost every Everest expedition since the 1920s, Sherpa porters and guides have carried bags, boxes, bottles of oxygen, portable stoves, tents, sleeping bags, crampons, drinking water, and snow goggles up and down Mount Everest on their backs. They have made tea and hot meals, put up tents, taken down tents, and led climbers to safety. They have fixed ladders and ropes, scouted routes, and selected campsites. They have buried the bodies of dead climbers. Some have been sickened or hurt on the treacherous mountain. Some have lost their lives in falls and avalanches.

Tenzing Norgay was one of the most experienced climbing Sherpas and had been on several other Himalayan expeditions, beginning in 1933. During the 1952 Swiss expedition, Norgay and team member Raymond Lambert climbed all the way to 28,200 feet (8,595 m), only about 800 feet (244 m) from the summit. This despite spending a night without sleeping bags and with barely any oxygen. They climbed higher than any known human had ever climbed before. But they were forced to turn around. They couldn't reach the summit before nightfall. Going ahead would have been too dangerous, and they couldn't last another night at that altitude.

Members of the 1953 Everest expedition pose for Gregory's camera.

Now the British had their turn. John Hunt was chosen as the leader for the 1953 British expedition. Hunt was a soldier who had already climbed several Himalayan mountains. He had a reputation for being efficient and determined, and as an outstanding organizer. He gathered a British team that embodied his four requirements: "age, temperament, experience, and physique; and I wanted a team," he said, "every member of which would be a potential 'summiter.'" Tom Bourdillon, a physicist, was asked to go since he was developing a more efficient oxygen apparatus to use on the mountain. Charles Wylie, an Army officer, looked after the porters and Sherpas. Charles Evans, a surgeon who had been to the Himalayas three times, was deputy leader. Wilfred Noyce, a teacher and writer who was also a climber, joined the team, as did Tom Stobart, who took the films of the expedition. *The London Times* sent a reporter, James Morris, who in later years was better known as travel writer Jan Morris. And there were two New Zealanders, Edmund Hillary, who was a beekeeper, and George Lowe, a schoolteacher and experienced climber. Hillary was one of the top mountaineers in his own country. In his book *Conquest of Everest,* Hunt writes that Hillary was "quite exceptionally strong and abounding in a restless energy, possessed of a thrusting mind which swept aside all unproved obstacles."

There was also Alfred Gregory, who at the age of 39 was the oldest member of the expedition except for

Alf Gregory was an experienced climber and photography enthusiast.

John Hunt. "Alf Gregory was ... small, neat and efficient, he knew how to conserve every bit of his strength and save it for the big moments," Edmund Hillary later wrote in an account of the expedition, *Nothing Venture, Nothing Win*. Gregory was to be in charge of the still photography for the expedition, although he was merely an amateur photographer. He later remembered the moment when he was chosen for that role at a meeting: "John Hunt looked around and said, 'Now who knows a bit about photography? Ah—Greg seems to take good pictures.'" Just like that, he was the expedition photographer.

Born in northern England, Gregory had been exploring and climbing hills since he was a teenager. He gradually progressed to climbing mountains, and by the time of the Everest expedition, he had spent several years climbing solo in the Alps, always with a keen amateur's interest in photography. In 1952, while the Swiss were attempting Everest, Gregory was invited on a trial run for Everest—a climb of Cho Oyu, the sixth highest mountain in the world, near Everest. Gregory excelled on the climb, cementing his place on the Everest team.

Once the group reached Nepal, they picked up Tenzing Norgay, completing the team of climbers. Hillary wrote in *Nothing Venture, Nothing Win* that he was eager to meet Norgay, whom he had heard a great deal about, and was impressed when he finally did: "Tenzing really looked the part [of the mountaineer]—larger than most Sherpas he was very strong and active; his flashing smile was

Gregory was to be in charge of the still photography for the expedition, although he was merely an amateur photographer.

MOUNT EVEREST'S THIN AIR

Hillary turns on Norgay's oxygen as they prepare to leave camp for their final climb.

Climbing a mountain is hard. Climbing a mountain in ice and snow, with constant risk of avalanches and falls, is harder. But anyone on Everest, including the 1953 team, also has to contend with extreme cold and the crippling, debilitating, sometimes fatal effects of extreme altitude.

The altitude problem on Everest is fairly simple: There is very little oxygen because the mountain is so high in the atmosphere. Climbers on Everest have to breathe harder just to get the same amount of oxygen a person gets when breathing at sea level. When a person breathes harder, he or she starts losing too much carbon dioxide. This makes a climber feel dizzy and lightheaded. It can make the climber faint, and it can even kill him or her.

An oxygen-starved climber can develop a condition called hypoxia—oxygen deprivation. Hypoxic people have no appetite and feel as if they have no energy. They have headaches, dizziness, nausea, vomiting, and fatigue. High on Everest, struggling with hypoxia, climbers feel as if it takes a great effort to make even ordinary movements.

People who are oxygen deprived can also have hallucinations and make dangerous errors in judgment, such as not fixing rope harnesses properly or simply walking off ledges above sheer rock faces. A modern climber remembered asking a companion with hypoxia to turn down his oxygen valve for him, and the companion, not thinking clearly, mistakenly turned the valve all the way up.

If a person living at sea level were to be airlifted to the top of Everest and placed there, he or she would lose consciousness from oxygen deprivation and die within minutes. If climbers take time and go slowly up the mountain, their bodies can get fairly used to using less oxygen. But at a certain altitude—about 2 miles (3.2 kilometers) *below* Everest's summit—people can never fully acclimate. In fact, if they stay above 20,000 feet (6,000 m) too long, according to the book *Everest: Mountain Without Mercy,* they face "a slow death by starvation, dehydration, suffocation, and exposure."

irresistible; and he was incredibly patient and obliging with all our questions and requests. His success in the past had given him great physical confidence."

With the team chosen, John Hunt made meticulous preparations, including the organizing of 5 tons (4.5 metric tons) of gear: thousands of feet of rope, ice axes, ice hammers, a 30-foot (9-m) sectional metal ladder, an avalanche gun to dislodge any lurking loose snow, windproof cotton-nylon outer suits, two-piece down inner suits. The team brought 12-man tents, two-man tents, nylon and down sleeping bags, air mattresses, cooking stoves, watches, radio equipment, sleeping pills, cigarettes, loose tobacco, stationery, lip salve, soap, batteries, flashlights, lanterns, compasses, and maps. The team also brought an impressive array of food: Grape-Nuts, coffee, cookies, canned soups, canned butter, nut and fruit bars, rum, oatmeal, tea, bouillon cubes, sausages, sugar, mix for scones, condensed milk, canned cake, glucose tablets, and a delicious-sounding Kendal mint cake, a type of energy bar. It's no wonder it took 350 porters plus yaks to haul the supplies over the foothills of Nepal to the base of Everest.

Oxygen systems were of particular concern to the team. High on Everest the air is so thin that most climbers must breathe bottled oxygen. At the time of the climb, there were two options, neither very good: open-circuit oxygen and closed-circuit. With the older, closed-circuit oxygen system, the climber breathed almost pure oxygen. But if the system malfunctioned

High on Everest the air is so thin that most climbers must breathe bottled oxygen.

A Sherpa carries a section of a ladder as he crosses a crevasse.

on the mountain, it was hard for the climber to adjust to the oxygen-scarce outside air. With the newer, open-circuit oxygen, the climber breathed some oxygen from the air tanks and some outside air. He was able to acclimate better, but he wasn't getting as much oxygen overall, making the climbing more difficult.

Finally the details of the journey were set. A few team members would fly to Kathmandu, the capital of Nepal. The rest would travel by ship to Bombay, India, now called Mumbai. All the team members and the baggage would assemble in Kathmandu. They would then trek overland by foot, with yaks carrying the supplies, to the foot of Everest, where they would establish their base camp.

They would spend about three weeks moving their stores from the base camp to progressively higher camps on Everest. This system would have two purposes: the only way to move such large amounts of equipment was to ferry them on one's back, so the gear had to be moved gradually and dumped at camps. Also, moving up and then down the mountain repeatedly over a long period of time gave the climbers' bodies a chance to acclimate to the altitude. Only after the high camps were established would the climbers begin their assault attempts.

Sherpas carry supplies to base camp at the foot of Everest. For the next three weeks supplies would be moved higher and higher up the mountain.

ChapterThree
THE ASSAULT

Most of the climbers left England for India on February 12 on the SS *Stratheden*, planning to use the long sea journey to rest. This team transported 473 packages, totaling 7.5 tons (6.8 metric tons), from the ship to a large train, then to a small train, then to trucks.

The rest of the men traveled by airplane, as planned, and the groups joined in Kathmandu, on March 8, to begin walking to Everest. First, though, they met with their Sherpas, led by Tenzing Norgay. "Tenzing's simplicity and gaiety quite charmed us, and we were quickly impressed by his authority in the role of Sirdar [head Sherpa]," John Hunt wrote in *Conquest of Everest*. Hunt also noted that there was so much luggage going on the trek that 12 porters were needed just to carry the chests of Nepali coins that would be used to pay the porters.

For 17 days the team made an idyllic 175-mile (282-km) trek through Nepal to the base of Everest. They walked through flower-filled valleys and lush forests and over foothills. Icy mountains in the distance grew steadily closer. They stopped sometimes to climb smaller peaks. Gregory took photographs of the trek, many of which later appeared in his book, *The Picture of Everest*. In his commentary, Gregory wrote: "This was the month of March, which is perhaps the most delightful period for a walk to the high mountains. At that time of the year the

"Tenzing's simplicity and gaiety quite charmed us, and we were quickly impressed by his authority in the role of Sirdar."

Dressed in shorts at the lower altitude, Edmund Hillary stops to gaze at the Himalayas during the trek to Everest.

countryside is a riot of colour. In the valleys flowers were growing all around us ... [Trees were] covered with almond blossom and always this sea of colour was set against a background of deep Himalayan forest."

Soon the landscape shifted and the mountains grew ever closer. At the end of March, Gregory writes, "After a short day's march ... we arrived at the Buddhist monastery of Thyangboche. ... The grassy alp is ringed with silver birches, azaleas, rhododendron bushes and fir trees, and beyond these in every direction tower ice peaks which for majesty of outline surely cannot be rivaled anywhere. ... We could never tire of looking at them and ... seeing the long streamers of snow-plume blowing from the high crests in the gale up there with the sun shining through, giving a feeling of a cold unapproachable world above us."

The team reached the base of Everest on April 12 and established their base camp. Gregory noted, "Here, amongst piles of stones on what from above looked like an island of moraine in the ice, was a cluster of yellow and pink tents and equipment waiting transport up the mountain. All around were enormous pinnacles of ice hiding the camp. ... This was our base from where all our climbing started and, although it was not a very comfortable place, it was a very welcome sight to parties returning from the higher camps."

Mount Everest is a vast mountain with several distinct parts. The huge Khumbu Glacier flows slowly down the mountain. In a valley at the base of Everest, the glacier

A British flag flies over Base Camp, which is surrounded by ice pinnacles.

laps out a tongue of notoriously unstable ice—the Khumbu Icefall. Here the ice piles up in huge towers called seracs. These ice blocks are merely balanced on each other and on the shifting tongue of ice, and they can collapse at any time. Some are the size of refrigerators, others as big as three-story houses. For the expedition the greatest challenge was ferrying supplies from Base Camp, just outside the icefall, to camps farther up the mountain. Gregory writes in *The Picture of Everest* about the Sherpas' carrying supplies up the mountain: "Their way was across a chaos of ice, threading through a

Mount Everest looms over the ice formations in the treacherous icefall.

labyrinth of tottering ice blocks, on ground that was never sure and almost always seemed to be hollow, so that the climber was moving over jammed blocks of ice above the abyss below."

The icefall dangers haven't changed much in 60 years. A modern climber writes: "The Khumbu glacier is ice under stress: creaking and bumping and clicking and snapping and cracking and squeaking—a constant babble. It's always reminding us that we're camping on a dynamic sheet of ice."

Massive crevasses snake through the icefall, opening

A Sherpa uses a rope ladder to climb an ice wall.

further as the ice shifts. The 1953 team used ropes and aluminum ladders placed precariously across the unstable abysses to go over them. They even cut small trees from much farther down in the valley, stripped them of branches and bark, hauled them up the mountain and fixed them in place as temporary ladders, secured by metal spikes driven into the ice. With his small camera, Gregory captured striking shots of goggled and hatted Sherpas placing tree trunks across crevasses. In another photo, a Sherpa climbs up a sheer ice wall, carrying an enormous box of oxygen bottles attached by a headband.

Once past the icefall, the climbers then and now

Sherpas cross the Western Cwm with Lhotse Face in the distance.

> **"Hard, frozen snow, glistening blue ice and stones form this plateau, swept almost continually by an Everest gale."**

encounter the Western Cwm, named by George Mallory. The Cwm (pronounced koom) is sometimes called the Valley of Silence, and even though it is very flat, it can be quite difficult to traverse: Solar radiation from the sun is intense here. When there is no wind, it can get intensely hot as the sun reflects off the dazzlingly white surfaces, making climbers pray for a breeze.

At the head of the Cwm, the team established their Advance Base Camp, the place they would use as a base during the assault attempt. Gregory wrote: "The rock bastion of Everest itself, massive in its strength, towered above our camp: a wall of granite that rose in a sweep of rock slab and buttress to the South Summit of Everest. It was up there that our eyes were mostly turned, to the point where a snow plume always blew."

To progress up Everest, climbers must fight their way up the Lhotse Face, 3,700 feet (1,128 m) of steep glacial ice. Then they encounter the South Col, a football-field-sized pass between Everest and Lhotse at 26,000 feet (7,925 m). It is the Advance Base Camp for most modern teams, with wicked winds that can knock down a tent in moments. "The South Col ... must be one of the most unpleasant spots in the world," Gregory wrote. "Here the altitude, the wind and the cold combine to make a vital, vicious force, a force that seems almost tangible in its reality, pressing down on the climber and making life unbearable. Hard, frozen snow, glistening blue ice and stones form this plateau, swept almost continually by an Everest gale."

A climber continuing up Everest then crosses the Southeast Ridge, a 1,000-foot (305 m) snow ridge that ends at the South Summit, which is a snow dome only 300 feet (91 m) below the summit. But the 1953 team wouldn't encounter these parts of Everest for another six weeks.

By the end of April the team had established two camps and was busy setting up Camp III at the top of the icefall. They were also getting to know each other even better. Edmund Hillary wrote on April 26 that he had had a chance to climb with Norgay for the first time: "I was impressed with his strength, his sound technique, and particularly his willingness to rush off on any variation I might suggest."

Norgay was also favorably impressed by Hillary. In his own memoir, *Tiger of the Snows*, he writes, "Hillary was a wonderful climber ... and had great strength and endurance. Like many men of action, and especially the British, he did not talk much, but he was, nevertheless, a fine, cheerful companion."

Conditions on the mountain were snowy and stormy. Many members of the team were struggling with exhaustion, but nonetheless, the team managed to establish seven camps stringing almost all the way up the mountain. Hunt had laid out the assault plan. There would be three attempts: Charles Evans and Tom Bourdillon would climb first, using the closed-circuit oxygen system. If they failed to summit, Norgay and Hillary would climb, using the open-circuit oxygen. If they failed, the team

"Hillary was a wonderful climber ... and had great strength and endurance."

Team members climb to Camp IV, one of seven established on the mountain.

would have time to send one more pair to try for the top.

Evans and Bourdillon left for their assault attempt May 26. But the trip didn't start well—they had trouble with their oxygen equipment early in the morning and departed later than they had intended. Gregory snapped a photo of the pair on their way up the mountain. By 11 o'clock, Evans was struggling with his oxygen again. Hillary wrote: "At 1 p.m. Tom and Charles disappeared over the South Summit—what an achievement!" Hillary and Norgay could see the men trudging up the mountain before the clouds concealed them.

At the South Summit, Evans was still struggling with his malfunctioning oxygen gear. But for the first time, he and Bourdillon had a close-up view of the final ridge leading to the summit. It was narrow, steep, and almost completely exposed, with drops of 8,000 feet (2,438 m) on one side and 10,500 feet (3,200 m) on the other. It would be very challenging to climb, and Evans had little oxygen.

They decided to retreat. By the time they made their way back to the South Col, they were utterly exhausted. Gregory captured a photo of them sitting on rocks in camp, heads down, hands dangling between their knees. They look spent. Hillary wrote that the men reported they had had a terrible time descending: "Absolutely exhausted, their descent of the ridge was hazardous in the extreme. They had a number of tumbles in tricky places and then fell from top to bottom of the great couloir [deep gorge]— it was a miracle they survived. They reached the South Col

Charles Evans (left) and Tom Bourdillon were exhausted after their retreat. Bourdillon always regretted the decision to turn back, but both men knew they would have run out of oxygen.

SUMMIT
SOUTH
SUMMIT

IX

VIII

VII

VI

To V

IV

III

II

BASE

From Base Camp
to the summit, a
series of camps
marked the route
to Everest's peak.

more exhausted than any men I have ever seen. Tom was still bitterly disappointed they hadn't tried for the top—but Charles knew they would never have returned. Too tired almost to talk, they painted a gloomy picture of the ridge running on towards the summit; and expressed their doubts about us making it."

Weather conditions were not good. It was very cold and the wind was kicking up. "Life on the Col was an

John Hunt (from left), Edmund Hillary, and Tenzing Norgay with support team members Ang Nyima, Alf Gregory, and George Lowe

extreme of misery," the usually understated Hillary wrote. By the next morning, May 27, Tom Bourdillon had not recovered from the attempt the day before. He couldn't descend under his own power, and Evans couldn't escort Bourdillon alone. One of the Sherpas, Ang Temba, was sick too. And John Hunt himself was very tired, though he didn't want to admit it. The group descended to Camp VII, leaving Hillary, Norgay, and the support team of Gregory, George Lowe, and Sherpa Ang Nyima high on

The Himalayas form a magnificent backdrop to Hillary and Norgay, on the verge of reaching Everest's summit.

With his Kodak Retina 2 camera, he snapped what *Photography Monthly* has called "one of the most significant photographs known to man."

the mountain, poised for the second assault attempt.

They set out on the morning of May 28 feeling strong and eager. Lowe and Gregory led the way, both carrying loads of about 40 pounds (18 kg) and cutting steps—slicing out boot-shaped areas in the hard snow. This would help Hillary and Norgay conserve their energy later—all they would have to do is follow the steps.

By now the team was very tired and struggled to find a place flat enough to pitch a tent for Hillary and Norgay. Finally at 27,900 feet (8,504 m), Norgay ranged a little off the path and found a spot just wide enough for one person to lie down and a platform about a foot below it for the other man. The tent could have a two-level floor. Gregory wrote, "There at 3 o'clock in the afternoon George Lowe, Ang Nyima and I turned to go down, leaving Ed Hillary and Tenzing to their lonely vigil of the night of May 28th."

But Gregory did another, very important thing before he left: With his Kodak Retina 2 camera, he snapped what *Photography Monthly* has called "one of the most significant photographs known to man."

He captured the two climbers poised on the mountain, on their way to sleep higher than any known human had slept before. Norgay stands in the foreground, his oxygen mask on his face, wearing a peach-colored parka and puffy gray snow pants. He is looking directly at the camera, his face and head all but obscured by his oxygen mask, snow goggles, and woolly hat. He braces his arms on his load, which sits on the snow in front of him. Visible are his blue windproof jacket, tied to the pack, two oxygen bottles on a metal frame—no doubt the open-circuit system they would use—and gear below.

Hillary stands upright just behind Norgay. He is wearing his blue wind jacket and a helmetlike down hood. He looks down slightly, and has pushed his mask to the side. His eyes are obscured by snow goggles, but the expression on his face is good-humored and calm, with a slight smile, as if he is enjoying a small joke.

Climbing ropes are around both men's waists. A large pink wrapped bundle is beside Hillary, part of his load. The men are standing on a small, level section of the mountain, with large rocks packed with snow scattered around them. Behind them spreads the vastness of the Himalayas, with snow-covered mountain peaks almost obscured by fog or mist.

For more than 30 years, climbers had been battling Everest. Norgay and Hillary, poised in their confident, casual way, were about to end the battle victoriously.

EXTREME PHOTOGRAPHY

Support team member George Lowe changes film in his camera at 27,300 feet (8,320 m).

"Taking pictures upwards of 25,000 feet, in fifty degrees of frost, often delicately balanced on difficult ground, with a murderous wind blowing, a heavy load on your back and an oxygen mask on your face, requires a good deal of resolve," John Hunt wrote.

On Everest Alfred Gregory did not just have the challenge of climbing and carrying heavy loads and taking striking, artistic photos in a hostile and oxygen-deprived environment. He also had to manage the mechanics of his camera and film. Gregory took a few small cameras with him on the journey—a Contax, a Rolleiflex and two Kodaks—that could be easily carried. No one knew how a camera would behave at extreme altitude and in extreme cold. Cameras in 1953 were entirely mechanically driven instead of electronic. This means that the shutter and the film advance were driven by tiny gears, and these gears needed to stay lubricated in order to function. Gregory feared the lubricant would freeze, rendering his camera useless. He also worried that the film would malfunction—no one knew how the delicate coating that made recording images possible would react to such extreme conditions. Plastic in the camera itself could freeze and simply shatter.

These potential problems turned out to be no trouble at all. Gregory took care to keep the cameras and film warm at all times by keeping them inside his clothing, against his body. At night he kept them inside his sleeping bag. The cameras worked beautifully.

ChapterFour
TRIUMPH!

Edmund Hillary and Tenzing Norgay settled in for the night of May 28 in their tent. "We had managed to flatten out the rocks and ice under the tent, but not at all one level," wrote Norgay in *Tiger of the Snows*. "Half the floor was about a foot higher than the other half, and now Hillary spread his sleeping bag on the upper shelf and I put mine on the lower." They ate chicken noodle soup, sardines, dates, and canned apricots. They drank many mugs of hot, sweet lemon water, which kept them hydrated and full of carbohydrates. They shared oxygen so they could sleep in shifts. At 3 in the morning, they woke to find that Hillary's boots had frozen solid. He had taken them off to sleep, while Norgay had kept his on. Hillary had to thaw them over their little stove for an hour. But at 6:30 a.m., Hillary wrote, "we moved off."

Very carefully, they traversed the dangerous snow ridge Bourdillon and Evans had warned them about, reaching the South Summit by 9 a.m. Then they found themselves at the base of a rocky spire about 40 feet (12 m) high. They could not go around it or climb straight up. They were stymied, until Hillary saw a cornice of ice wedged against the rock. It had melted some, giving footholds. He thought of wedging himself between the ice and the rock and shimmying up. There was a risk that the ice would give way. But he would have to take it—it was

> At 3 in the morning, they woke to find that Hillary's boots had frozen solid.

The first of several tents set up at Camp VII, where the support team waited for Hillary and Norgay to return from the summit.

On the summit of Everest, Norgay waves his ice ax bearing the flags of Great Britain, Nepal, the United Nations, and India.

"Immediately it was obvious that we had reached our objective. It was 11:30 a.m. and we were on top of Everest!"

either that or give up, because there was no other option.

The ice held as they wormed their way up. They crossed another ridge, though not as steep. "I continued on," Hillary wrote, "cutting [steps] steadily and surmounting bump after bump and cornice after cornice looking eagerly for the summit. ... Finally I cut around the back of an extra large hump and then on a tight rope from Tenzing I climbed up a gentle snow ridge to its top. Immediately it was obvious that we had reached our objective. It was 11:30 a.m. and we were on top of Everest!"

"[T]he sky was the deepest blue I have ever seen," Norgay wrote. "Only a gentle breeze was blowing. ... At that great moment for which I had waited all my life my mountain did not seem to me a lifeless thing of rock and ice, but warm and friendly and living."

Hillary and Norgay hugged each other and planted an ice ax with the flags of the United Nations, Britain, Nepal, and India. Hillary took photographs with his small Kodak camera and they buried some sweets, a little pencil from Norgay's daughter, and a little cloth cat from Hunt. To celebrate, they ate some of the Kendal mint cake they had brought. Then they made their way back down.

The next morning the *Times* correspondent James Morris sent the news to London via a coded message. Gregory's exposed film was sewn into a canvas bag, carried down to Base Camp, and sent by runner to the British Embassy in Kathmandu. From there it was flown to

Hillary and Norgay back at Camp IV after their successful assault of Mount Everest.

London. The triumphant news broke in Britain on the new Queen Elizabeth's Coronation Day, June 2.

The team was greeted as heroes when they landed at London's Heathrow Airport. Some people thought their success reaffirmed the greatness of England's power. *The New York Times* declared: "The magnificent feat of the British expedition will no doubt be taken by many of Her Majesty's loyal subjects as an omen that England is indeed

DISPATCH FROM 1953

Expedition members cross the Western Cwm. Behind them stands Mount Lingtren at 21,972 feet (6,697 m).

On June 7, 1953, just days after the summit was reached, *The New York Times* wrote of the triumph, describing the hardship and speculating about the team's motivations. At the time climbers were still debating whether using oxygen on a mountain was cheating, a controversy noted in the article: "The conquest of Mount Everest shared the front page last week with the Coronation [of Queen Elizabeth II]. And deservedly so. Since 1921 more than a dozen expeditions have gasped for breath, when they were not inhaling oxygen, and took steps as deliberate and slow as if they were marching in a funeral procession as they climbed the world's highest mountain. In fact, the taking of a step near the summit was an athletic feat, to be followed by a rest. Fifteen men have died on the slopes of Mount Everest.

"... Perfectionists among [climbers] consider it unsportsmanlike to rely on anything but natural breathing, no matter how high a peak may be. But it is certain that without oxygen Mount Everest and peaks almost as high would never be climbed. Even with oxygen tanks to draw upon, the upward struggle is not greatly simplified. Men have to overcome their lethargy, their indifference to what may happen, their illusions of well-being. Sometimes a man who badly needs oxygen will stare at a tank of it and wonder what it is for. The conquest of Mount Everest is a conquest of man as well as of a mountain.

"Why do men want to climb the world's highest mountain and suffer such hardships? There is no gold or other precious mineral on top of Everest, nothing that arouses [greed], no important scientific advantage that cannot be gained more easily with an airplane. We have to fall back on man's unquenchable thirst for adventure and the daredevil in him."

Hillary snapped a photo from the summit looking west. The panoramic view showcases Mounts Pumori, Cho Oyu, Lingtren, and the West Rongbuk Glacier.

entering a new Elizabethan Age, an age of greatness in which British might and British valor will once more conquer the unconquerable."

But *Time* magazine has pointed out that reaching the Everest summit "was more an ending. Hillary and Tenzing's accomplishment was the last major earthly adventure and also the last great symbol of Empire. The next great exploratory leap came with a push into

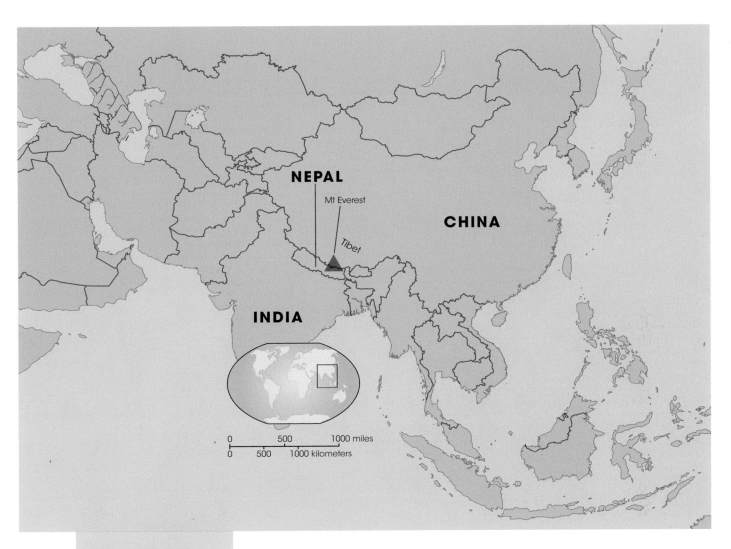

Mount Everest, the world's tallest mountain, lies on the border of Nepal and Tibet.

space by the new superpowers: the Soviet Union and the United States."

Whatever the greater meaning of the expedition, one thing is clear: Gregory's photos, including the one of Hillary and Norgay poised near the summit, offered the world a glimpse into a hidden universe, a glimpse that the team alone had seen. And the team felt keenly their duty to share this special place. Hunt wrote: "It seemed to me that we, who were to have this wonderful experience of

Hillary took a photo of the footprints he and Norgay left in the snow on their way down from Everest's summit.

travelling through a beautiful and comparatively unknown land and penetrating into a rugged, ice-gripped waste towards the top of the world, had a certain responsibility to those others, not so fortunate but no less fascinated by our opportunity. The best way to help them share it with us ... was to bring back a fine collection of pictures. It was for this reason we took great pains about our still photography."

Many, many expeditions have been on Mount Everest since that day in 1953. About 4,000 people have reached the summit. Mount Everest is no longer unknown. But as art critic Sebastian Smee wrote in the *Telegraph* of London in 2003, "When Alfred Gregory took this photograph on Mount Everest 50 years ago, he had taken his camera higher than anyone had previously taken one without flying. It is hard to imagine an image more exact, or—in terms of the human drama that it depicts—egalitarian." Two men, a team, and a mountain. An adventure pared down to bare bones.

Edmund Hillary lived a life of fame after Everest, writing many books and articles. He received a knighthood from Queen Elizabeth and went on to be the first person to reach the South Pole by motorized vehicle. He traveled up the Ganges and through the rivers of Nepal. But he spent most of his later years raising money to benefit the people of rural Nepal and building schools and a hospital there. He became the ambassador to Nepal from New Zealand. And Hillary passed on his mountaineering genes. In 1990 his son Peter Hillary had the thrill of calling his father

Norgay, 39, and Hillary, 33, at the Thyangboche Monastery on the trek back to Kathmandu

from the summit of Everest. Edmund Hillary lived a long life and met a peaceful end, dying of heart failure in 2008 at the age of 88.

Tenzing Norgay was also catapulted to immediate fame in Nepal and around the world. Queen Elizabeth awarded him the George Medal, given to people who have performed acts of great courage. He kept his natural humbleness, though, and went on to become the director of field training at the Himalayan Mountaineering Institute in Darjeeling, India. He lived quietly within

"Everest was once the loneliest mountain on earth," wrote Alfred Gregory. "Until we broke the silence."

view of Everest for the rest of his life and died of a lung infection five days shy of 72.

As for Alfred Gregory, he never left adventure or photography after the Everest expedition, although eventually he did leave the mountains. "I went to Everest a keen amateur photographer but I came back a 'pro'," Gregory said. A famous pro, he could have added. Gregory traveled and lectured for the Eastman Kodak Company, talking about the expedition. He worked as a freelance photographer and ran a trekking company, leading alpine

Alfred Gregory at work on the Everest expedition; he died at age 96 in 2010.

expeditions. He took other famous photographs, especially those documenting life in the swinging tourist town of Blackpool, England, in the 1960s. He settled in Australia but traveled the world, photographing native people in many countries.

Gregory also lived a long time and, as the years went on, he watched more and more groups swarm Everest. The teams left huge amounts of litter, desecrating the mountain, Gregory felt. He disliked the modern system of guided tours to Everest. "I tried to photograph the silence of Everest," he told *Australian Geographic*. "The South Col was a pristine wilderness with no footprints on it at all. Just the South Summit lost in the high cloud ... This is how I like to remember it—before the commercialisation of the mountain, before the advent of the hordes and their litter."

And because of Gregory—and all the members of the 1953 expedition—the rest of the world also can experience the silence of Everest.

Timeline

1856

The Great Trigonometrical Survey of British India maps Mount Everest and finds that, at just over 29,000 feet (8,840 m), it is the highest place on Earth; called Peak XV, it is later named after George Everest, former surveyor general of India

1921

The British organize the first reconnaissance expedition to Everest, which includes climber George Mallory; a northern route is explored

1950

Tibet—now under Chinese control—closes its borders to foreigners, shutting off Everest's northern route

1951

Nepal's borders are opened to foreign visitors; another British reconnaissance expedition explores the southern route, which is accessible from Nepal

1923

A newspaper reporter asks Mallory why he wants to climb Mount Everest; "Because it is there" is his famous reply

1924

Mallory and Andrew Irvine disappear high on Everest during a summit attempt

1952

A Swiss expedition makes two summit attempts; Raymond Lambert and Tenzing Norgay reach the Southeast Ridge and are forced to turn around 800 feet (244 m) from the summit; British and New Zealand climbers, including Alfred Gregory, Tom Bourdillon, George Lowe, Charles Evans, and Edmund Hillary, climb the Himalayan mountain Cho Oyu in preparation for Mount Everest, but don't reach the summit

September 1952

John Hunt takes his place as leader of the 1953 expedition

Timeline

November 1952

A leadership committee, with Hunt's recommendations, chooses the British and New Zealand climbing team members

February 1953

The team leaves England for India; two members, Evans and Gregory, travel by air February 20 as an advance party; Hunt and Bourdillon fly out a week later, and the rest travel by ship

May 17, 1953

The seventh main camp is established on Everest, paving the way for the summit attempts

May 26, 1953

Bourdillon and Evans reach the South Summit in the first assault attempt; they are forced to retreat

May 28, 1953

Hillary and Norgay ascend to their high camp in preparation for the second assault attempt, supported by Lowe, Gregory, and Ang Nyima

March 1953

Tenzing Norgay is added as a climbing team member; the entire team leaves Kathmandu to begin the trek to Everest

April 1953

The team arrives at Everest and establishes Base Camp

May 29, 1953

Hillary and Norgay make the first known successful ascent of Everest

June 2, 1953

The entire team assembles at Base Camp to begin the trek back to Kathmandu; news of the ascent breaks in England on Queen Elizabeth's Coronation Day

Glossary

abyss—a hole so deep it seems impossible to measure

acclimate—the adaptation of a human body to a new environment, such as the scarce oxygen high on a mountain

altitude—the height of an object above sea level or ground level

cornice—mass of windblown snow or ice projecting over the edge of a mountain ridge

crampon—metal spikes that climbers attach over their boots to create a better grip

crevasse—crack in the surface of a glacier, which may be very wide or deep

cwm (koom)—Welsh word meaning bowl-shaped valley

debilitating—making weak or feeble

ice ax—climbing tool with a spike on one end and a head the shape of a pick on the other

icefall—unstable blocks of ice and crevasses that form when a glacier flows down a steep slope or pours out over a cliff

serac—pinnacle, sharp ridge, or block of ice on a glacier

sirdar—the leader of a group of Sherpa mountain guides and porters

yak—large hairy oxen used as a pack animal

Additional Resources

Further Reading

Chester, Jonathan. *The Young Adventurers' Guide to Everest: From Avalanche to Zopkio*. Berkeley, Calif.: Tricycle Press, 2005.

Kerr, Jim. *Hillary and Norgay's Mount Everest Adventure*. Chicago: Heinemann Library, 2008.

Whipple, Heather. *Hillary and Norgay: To the Top of Mount Everest*. New York: Crabtree Pub. Co., 2007.

Internet Sites

Use FactHound to find Internet sites related to this book. All of the sites on FactHound have been researched by our staff.

Here's all you do:
Visit *www.facthound.com*
Type in this code: 9780756547349

Critical Thinking Using the Common Core

The 1953 Everest group functioned as a team. Identify the various ways the group broke into teams throughout the expedition, and discuss how teamwork was crucial to the successful summit attempt. (Key Ideas and Details)

Throughout the mountaineering history of Everest, there has been a clear division between the roles of climbers and Sherpa porters. How would the story be told from a Sherpa point of view? (Craft and Structure)

John Hunt, the leader of the Everest expedition, said the team had a responsibility to bring back photos of the unknown world of Everest to share. Do you agree or disagree with Hunt's statement? Do photographers always have a responsibility to the public to share their photos? Explain why you do or do not agree. (Integration of Knowledge and Ideas)

Source Notes

Page 8, line 7: Jefferson Penberthy. "Climbing Into History." *Australian Geographic*. October–December 2007, p. 86.

Page 8, line 20: Alfred Gregory. *The Picture of Everest*. New York: E.P. Dutton and Co., 1954, unnumbered, "Hillary and Tenzing at Nearly 28,000 Feet."

Page 10, line 15: Ibid., "Introduction."

Page 16, line 7: John Hunt. *The Conquest of Everest*. New York: E.P. Dutton and Co., 1954, p. 24.

Page 17, line 10: Ibid., page 28.

Page 18, line 1: Edmund Hillary. *Nothing Venture, Nothing Win*. New York: Coward, McCann and Geoghegan, 1975, p. 146.

Page 18, line 8: Stephen Venables. "Alfred Gregory: Official photographer on the 1953 Everest expedition." *The Independent*. 10 Feb. 2010. 4 Oct. 2013. http://www.independent.co.uk/news/obituaries/alfred-gregory-official-photographer-on-the-1953-everest-expedition-1894230.html

Page 18, line 26: *Nothing Venture, Nothing Win*, p. 145.

Page 19, col. 2, line 19: Broughton Coburn. *Everest: Mountain Without Mercy*. Washington, D.C.: National Geographic Society, 1997, p. 127.

Page 24, line 9: *The Conquest of Everest*, p.61.

Page 24, line 23: *The Picture of Everest*, unnumbered, "A Valley in Nepal."

Page 26, line 6: Ibid., unnumbered, "Thyangboche."

Page 26, line 17: Ibid., unnumbered, "Base Camp."

Page 27, line 11: Ibid., unnumbered, "The Icefall."

Page 28, line 6: *Everest: Mountain Without Mercy*, p. 100.

Page 31, line 10: *The Picture of Everest*, unnumbered, "Camp Four."

Page 31, line 22: Ibid., unnumbered, "The South Col."

Page 32, line 11: *Nothing Venture, Nothing Win*, p. 151.

Page 32, line 16: Tenzing Norgay and James Ramsey Ullman. *Tiger of the Snows*. New York: G.P. Putnam's Sons, 1955, pp. 221–222.

Page 34, line 8: *Nothing Venture, Nothing Win*, p. 157.

Page 34, line 24: Ibid.

Page 36, line 8: Ibid.

Page 39, line 14: *The Picture of Everest*, unnumbered, "Hillary and Tenzing at Nearly 28,000 Feet."

Page 39, line 19: Earl Carter. "Alfred Gregory: Inspiring mountain photographer profiled." *Photography Monthly*. 19 July 2010. 4 Oct. 2013. http://www.photographymonthly.com/Tips-and-Techniques/Pro-Zone/Alfred-Gregory-inspiring-mountain-photographer-profiled

Page 41, line 1: *The Picture of Everest*, unnumbered, "Forward."

Page 42, line 2: *Tiger of the Snows*, p. 240.

Page 42, line 15: *Nothing Venture, Nothing Win*, p. 159.

Page 45, line 3: Ibid., pp. 160–161.

Page 45, line 12: *Tiger of the Snows*, pp. 249–250.

Page 46, line 6: "Conquest of Everest." *The New York Times*. 2 June 1953, p. 28. 4 Oct. 2013. http://query.nytimes.com/mem/archive/pdf?res=FA0C16F83D5B177B93C0A9178DD85F478585F9

Page 47, line 6: W.K. "Man's Conquest of the Highest Peak." *The New York Times*. 7 June 1953, p. E11. 4 Oct. 2013. http://query.nytimes.com/mem/archive/pdf?res=F10815FA3C5A117A93C5A9178DD85F478585F9

Page 48, line 5: Simon Robinson. "Sir Edmund Hillary: Top of the World." 10 Jan. 2008. 4 Oct. 2013. *Time*. http://www.time.com/time/world/article/0,8599,1702543-1,00.html

Page 49, line 8: *The Picture of Everest*, unnumbered, "Forward."

Page 51, line 13: Sebastian Smee. "Viewfinder: Alfred Gregory's Everest." *The Telegraph*. 3 May 2003. 4 Oct. 2013. http://www.telegraph.co.uk/culture/art/3593787/Viewfinder-Alfred-Gregorys-Everest.html

Page 53, caption: Alfred Gregory. *Alfred Gregory's Everest*. London: Constable and Co. Ltd., 1993, unnumbered, following page 175.

Page 53, line 5: Ibid., p. 29.

Page 55, line 10: "Climbing Into History," p. 86.

Select Bibliography

"Alf Gregory." *The Telegraph*. 10 Feb. 2010. http://www.telegraph.co.uk/news/obituaries/7207734/Alf-Gregory.html

Carter, Earl. "Alfred Gregory: Inspiring Mountain Photographer Profiled." *Photography Monthly*. 19 July 2010. http://www.photographymonthly.com/Tips-and-Techniques/Pro-Zone/Alfred-Gregory-inspiring-mountain-photographer-profiled

Coburn, Broughton. *Everest: Mountain Without Mercy*. Washington, D.C.: National Geographic Society, 1997.

"Conquest of Everest." *The New York Times*. 2 June 1953, p. 28.

"Everest." Nova Online: Everest. http://www.pbs.org/wgbh/nova/everest/climb/

Gilman, Peter, ed. *Everest: The Best Writing and Pictures from Seventy Years of Human Endeavour*. Boston: Little, Brown and Co. 1993.

Gregory, Alfred. *Alfred Gregory's Everest*. London: Constable and Co. Ltd., 1993.

Gregory, Alfred. *The Picture of Everest*. New York: E.P. Dutton and Co., 1954.

Handwerk, Brian. "The Sherpas of Mount Everest." *National Geographic News*. 10 May 2002. http://news.nationalgeographic.com/news/2002/05/0507_020507_sherpas.html

Hillary, Edmund. *Nothing Venture, Nothing Win*. New York: Coward, McCann and Geoghegan, 1975.

Hunt, John. *The Conquest of Everest*. New York: E.P. Dutton and Co., 1954.

Kraukauer, Jon. *Into Thin Air: A Personal Account of the Mount Everest Disaster*. New York: Random House, 1997.

Morris, James. *Coronation Everest*. New York: Dutton, 1958.

Norgay, Tenzing, and James Ramsey Ullman. *Tiger of the Snows*. New York: G.P. Putnam's Sons, 1955.

Penberthy, Jefferson. "Climbing Into History." *Australian Geographic*. October-December 2007, p. 86.

Robinson, Simon. "Sir Edmund Hillary: Top of the World." *Time*. 10 Jan. 2008. http://www.time.com/time/world/article/0,8599,1702543-1,00.html

Smee, Sebastian. "Viewfinder: Alfred Gregory's Everest." *The Telegraph*. 3 May 2003. http://www.telegraph.co.uk/culture/art/3593787/Viewfinder-Alfred-Gregorys-Everest.html

Tenzing, Tashi. *Tenzing Norgay and the Sherpas of Everest*. New York: Ragged Mountain Press, 2001.

"Traveling on Ice." WildernessSurvival. http://www.wilderness-survival.net/movement-snow-ice/ice-travel/

Unsworth, Walt. *Everest: A Mountaineering History*. Boston: Houghton Mifflin, 1981.

Venables, Stephen. "Alfred Gregory: Official Photographer on the 1953 Everest Expedition." *The Independent*. 10 Feb. 2010. http://www.independent.co.uk/news/obituaries/alfred-gregory-official-photographer-on-the-1953-everest-expedition-1894230.html

Venables, Stephen. *Everest: Summit of Achievement*. New York: Simon & Schuster, 2003.

W.K. "Man's Conquest of the Highest Peak." *The New York Times*. 7 June 1953, p. E11.

Index

About the Author

Emma Carlson Berne has written numerous historical and biographical books for children and young adults, as well as young adult fiction. She lives in Cincinnati with her husband and two sons.